RESOLVING YOUR DEBT/CREDIT CRISIS

RESOLVING YOUR DEBT/CREDIT CRISIS

Annie Nell Shephard

Library of Congress Control Number: 2015912241
ISBN: Hardcover   978-1-5035-9075-5
                 Softcover   978-1-5035-9077-9
                 eBook   978-1-5035-9076-2

Print information available on the last page.

Rev. date: 08/19/2015

To order additional copies of this book, contact:
Xlibris
1-888-795-4274
www.Xlibris.com
Orders@Xlibris.com
709561

CONTENTS

Maybe you are tired of robbing Peter to pay Paul, and Peter is tired too! Maybe you want to put an end to the debt collection agencies calling you. Maybe you need your credit repaired, or need help stopping foreclosure. Maybe you want to be able to get credit when your credit scores won't afford you credit. Or maybe you just want to pay off your mortgage early or just get out of debt; there is a chapter, just for you.

ABOUT THE AUTHOR

During the pregnancy of my first son, I realized that I wanted to be a full time mom, a part time worker, with full time pay. I was lead to the field of financial services. I have held license in the fields of Securities, Life Insurance, Health Insurance, Loan Originator, Mobile Home Sales Rep, and Mortgage Broker. Through these licenses, and my own personal experiences, I have gained valuable knowledge and expertise in the area of credit score enhancement, debt management and counseling.

From the early 90's to present, I have experienced my own personal highs and lows of financial success. My income went from six figures to zero. I had to deal with the constant harassment from creditors, and all the negative fallout of having poor credit. I educated myself on client's rights, consulted with the credit bureaus, and negotiated with creditors to repair my credit.

The market turndown during 2007 brought me to another low. By 2009 I found myself in the midst of my "perfect storm"; resources depleted and current profession on life support. I found myself again dealing with debt collectors, struggling to keep my sons in college and staying one step ahead of having my car repossessed. At the end of 2011 the storm, as if it could not get any worse, did intensify, our home and all our belongings were lost to a fire. I was mentally devastated and stifled. The year 2013 brought the loss of my mother that only extended my mental inability to start over. The year 2014 for me as a new beginning. I could continue to wallow in my past situations or start over again. I chose to start over again.

I share this with you because I want you, to know that I understand and have experienced firsthand what you are going through. There is Hope and there is a way up!

I bring to my readers over thirty years of experience in the world of finances and hard knocks. I have gone from financial feast to financial famine. I have shown countless people how to go from debt devastation to debt freedom and renters to homeowners. I am an example of not allowing any crisis to condemn you to a life of eternal struggle.

DEDICATIONS

First and foremost I thank God for allowing the valley experiences that have been a part of my life. Without those experiences I could not testify to the power of prayer and the goodness of God. To my mother, who went home to be with the Lord at the age of 97, Margaret Swain, who through her example, taught me that there is no such thing as can't, and that prayer will move any mountain. To my two sons Austin and Aasen, who have been my encourager, my shoulder to lean on, and at times, my legs to stand with, and above all, my purpose. To my sister Dianne Forbes and her family, and my niece Andrea Ashley and her family, for the love, help and support you have shown through my life crisis, I thank you and I love you all so very much.

To all my sisters or brothers, whether brown eyed, blue eyed, green eyed or any combination thereof; when hard times come remember, you, with the help of God, can overcome all situations if you will just "do it"!. You work hard every day trying to make ends meet and provide for your family. Setbacks will occur, but your Father knows what you have need of and He will provide. Be patient, stay prayed up, and joy will reveal itself in the morning. Choose to turn can't and how, into can and which way God? Regardless of your present position, you can and will achieve the things that appear unachievable.

BEFORE YOU BEGIN

I will not belabor you with the overwhelming facts of the American debt crisis. You brought this book to find out about your debt crisis and what you can do about it. You can start at the beginning, or jump into the chapter that deals with your immediate concerns.

To begin I need you to ask yourself several questions. Have you maintained your life style amassing debt to satisfy your desires? Have you conducted your life with the philosophy "I make enough money to make those payments", and never considered the total amount of debt you had generated for you and your family? Are you part of the "I gotta have it now" generation? Did you suddenly wake up one morning and realize that you have *"charged"* your future beyond your present ability to live comfortably? Are you so overwhelmed by your current amount of consumer debt that you are now checking the caller ID before you answer the phone? When you do answer the phone, do you find yourself making monthly un-kept promises to pay? Are you one step away from losing your home or cars, and the idea of bankruptcy really, really looks appealing? Did you build your lifestyles as a two income family and now there is only one income?

If you see yourself in any of the aforementioned descriptions, this book is for you. You need to know what happened so you don't take the same "crisis ridden" path again. The situation you are in did not happen overnight, and you are not going to correct it overnight. However, within the next several pages, I am going to show you how to achieve peace of mind, correct your current situation over time, and get back on track.

I encourage you to fix your eyes on where you are going and stop waddling in your current misfortune. Stop the pity parties now! Let us put together your plan of action and work the plan. I pray for your success with the help found in the following pages.

CHAPTER 1

YOUR DEBT CRISIS

To begin this journey of resolving your debt crisis, you must first know where you are. Once you know where you are you will be able to know in what direction you need to go, and when you are going to get to your goal of manageable debt.

To get started with the "where am I", you must generate a "Debt/ Expense Worksheet". List who you owe, how much, and what are the monthly payments. Make this list in order of priority; you're most important bill, what you don't want to lose, and so on. When detailing expenses, list everything! Be very detailed, list any and all things you spend money on routinely during the week. Once you have completed the list, total each column. Subtract your total payments from your total **take home pay**. The result will show you what your shortfall is, how much money you don't have at the end of the month.

No matter how overwhelming your shortfall is, if you have a plan, and follow the plan, you will resolve your debt crisis. An example follows.

Debts and Expenses

	Debt/Expenses	Owe($)	Payment($)
	Total Take Home Pay		**$4,560.50**
1.	Tithe		456.05
2.	*Mortgage	155,000	979.71
3.	2nd Mtg.	25,000	300.04
4.	Car #1	26,000	642.95
5.	Car #2	18,000	439.43
6.	Car Ins.		130.00
7.	Life Ins.		100.00
8.	Food/home supplies		500.00
9.	Utilities		200.00
10.	Gas		320.00
11.	Loan	5,000	146.87
12.	Miscellaneous		300.00
13.	Credit Card #1	10,000	250.00
14.	Card #2	7,000	140.00
15.	Gas Card #1	1,000	27.50
16.	Gas Card #2	1,200	33.00
17.	Store Credit Card #1	7,000	175.00
18.	Store Credit Card #2	1,500	37.50
19.	Gym		50.00
	Total(s)	$256,700	$5,228.05
	Take home pay minus debt		-$667.55

In this scenario you have $667.55 more debt/expenses than you have money. You have a DEBT CRISIS!

The next step in the process is to get a plan as to what your take home pay will allow you to pay. Please note I said take home pay, you don't live off your gross income. Let's assume for this example, that the individual can pay debts one through twelve. This scenario leaves seven creditors that you do not have the ability to pay each month.

To resolve your shortfall you should first look at creating part-time income. Secondly, contact your creditors for items one through twelve, to see if you can work out a lower monthly payment. The lowering of the payments may allow you to incorporate another debts to be paid monthly. However, if you have exhausted all options and still have a shortfall, you must generate a "Pay-U-Latter List"

The "Pay-U-Latter List" is a list of creditors who you no longer have the ability to pay. Identifying who goes on your list is not that difficult. You decide who does not get paid by one rule. "If they can't come get it, I can't pay it"; or "If you don't care if they come get it, I can't pay it". Once you identify who goes on your Pay-U-Latter list, you must now communicate with those creditors and send them the "I'm sorry letter".

Write each creditor on the "Pay-U-Latter List" and express your regret for your inability to pay them at this time. (This letter, if written properly, will also stop the harassing phone calls.) Along with your regrets, you will instruct them "that under the Fair Debt Collection Pratices Act, they are not to call you regarding this matter". Send the letter via certified or registered mail, and mail yourself a copy. When you receive your copy do not open it, just file it. If they call you after you have received confirmation that they received your letter, you can report them to the Federal Trade Commission. Remember, you owe the debt, and when your financial picture improves make arrangements to pay them. An example of the "I'm sorry letter" follows.

Dear Creditor,

I am writing you regarding my account, # xxxxxx. This letter is to inform you that due to my recent job lost, (or whatever your situation is) I am no longer able to make the agreed upon payments. I realize I do owe this debt, but circumstances do not allow me to make any payments at this time.

I am requesting, Under the Fair Debt Collection Practices Act, that you no longer contact me, my family members or friends, regarding this debt. Please do not contact me at work, on my cell phone, or home phone regarding this debt. If you turn this debt over to a collection agency, I am requesting that you attach this letter to the file.

When I am in position to pay this debt I will. Pleases accept my sincere apologies for not being able to honor the financial trust you extended to me.

Sincerely,

Even though you are delinquent on a debt, you still have rights as a consumer. Those rights for individuals that owe creditors but are unable to pay, fall under the Fair Debt Collection Practices Act. (**It would be well worth your time to go on-line and read this Act, www. fcra.com**.)

If possible, always try to work out a reduced payment with your creditor. Most creditors are willing to work with you. When you call to make an agreement for lower payments, know that you can honor that arrangement. **Don't agree to pay more than your money will allow. Don't allow yourself to be pushed to a higher payment that you cannot afford. You are working on resolving your debt crisis not creating new ones. By making promises to pay what is not doable with your take home pay, is only creating new crises.**

Your Debt/Expense worksheet now becomes your new budget. When you are ready to budget, detail your miscellaneous expenses.

Under the miscellaneous expense add in a Emergency Fund. I realize when you are stretched to your financial limit, a savings does not seem reasonable, however it is a must. At this point in the process you may only be able to save $10.00 a month, but save that $10.00 a month consistently. You don't know what financial challenges may be around the corner. The more prepared you are, the less effect a storm can have on your life. Your short term goal with this emergency fund is getting it to $1,000.00. Your long term goal with this emergency fund is to save to the point that it contains an amount equal to 6-12 months of you new budget. The needed amount may appear overwhelming, but start with whatever you can set aside each month and be consistent. This Emergency Fund is a do not touch account except for emergencies. The example that follows shows your needs every month and how you can manage them.

BUDGET EXAMPLE

	Debt	Sch. Pymt	Jan	Feb	Mar	Apr	May	Jun	Total
1	Tithes	456	456	456					
2	Mortgage	979.71	980	980					
3	2nd Mtg	300.04	301	301					
4	Car 1	642.95	643	643					
5	Car 2	439.43	440	440					
6	Car Ins.	130	130	130					
7	Life Ins.	100	100	100					
8	Food/supplies	600	550	450					
9	Electric	200	195	190					
10	Gas	320	200	195					
11	Loan	146.87	147	147					
12	Hair Care	60	30	0					
13	Car Gas	120	145	145					
14	Parking	75	75	75					
15	Cell	130	130	130					
16	Emergency Fund	50	20	50					
	Total paid	4750	4397	4257					
	Total Income	4550	4550	4550					
	Residual Income	-200	+153	+263					

A budget is very easy to make, the challenge is sticking to it. If you have a family, you need to make sure you involve everyone when it comes to making your budget. Review monthly with your family to keep everyone abreast of the families progress. To move out your crisis, you must stick to your budget.

Because you are in a crisis, you and your family members, need to search for ways to reduce your monthly expenses. Here are some things to consider to reduce your monthly expenses and increase your residual income.

Increasing Your Residual Income

1. Look at your phone(s) and change carriers or plans. Eliminate all frills from your plan.
2. If possible, eliminate the home phone if everyone has a cell.
3. Look at your cable bill - go basic, change carriers or cancel.
4. Plan your menus each week before you go shopping, and make your grocery list from the menu. If it's not on the grocery list it does not go in the cart.
5. Team up with a neighbor or family member and buy in bulk common household items.
6. Start a garden; grow your own bell peppers, tomatoes, seasonings, etc.
7. Clip coupons.
8. Many groceries stores mark down meats in the morning. Speak to your butcher find out what time they do the mark downs. You will be surprised at your savings.
9. When cooking, cook for more than 1 day and build on the left over's. For example, you have rice chicken and vegetables. After one or two days you may have a little rice or even vegetables left, your next meal could be stuffed bell peppers in which you incorporate the rice and vegetables.
10. Coordinate your trips to minimize gas usage. Carpool to work and events if possible.

11. Keep up the maintenance on your cars; it will cost you less in the long run.
12. Perform all car maintenance that you can do yourself.
13. Look at the cost of your various insurance policies. Look for the same coverage at a lower price. If you have a life insurance policy that is whole life, or universal life, you can probably reduce your cost by switching to a Term life insurance policy.
14. Shop at thrift stores, yard sales, and consignment shops for clothing and household items, you will save a fortune.
15. If you usually get a huge tax refund every year you are allowing the government to hold your money for twelve months without any interest. Increase your exemptions on your W-9 at work. This will give you more in your paycheck when you need it, which is now!
16. Take your lunch to work and school.
17. Change the frequency that you go to the barber or salon. If possible do it yourself.
18. Make sure your family members are aware of the situation and talk about ways that expenses can be reduced. Talk about turning lights off when not in use, change the setting on your heat/air.
19. Cancel your newspaper and magazine subscriptions.
20. Don't let pride hinder you from seeking help. Churches have food banks and they give out food weekly. Don't be too proud to accept this food, it will help lower your food bill.
21. See if you qualify for food stamps.
22. Get a part-time job or start a business.
23. Use fans at night during the summer. Speak with your electric company about cost. Speak to your electric or gas company about ways to reduce your cost.
24. Unplug everything that is not in use
25. Reuse the bags from the grocery store as trash bags.
26. Buy light bulbs that have a longer life. They may cost more in the beginning but they generate savings in the long run.

27. Stop eating pre-packaged foods, they cost more. Find the time to make the pancakes and waffles vs. buying frozen.
28. Go to the movies during the day. Cheaper tickets.

If you just told yourself "I don't have time for all these things". Look at the consequence of not taking the time to change!

Check-up:

Up to this point you have:
1. Identified how you arrived at your debt crisis.
2. Identified what debts you are able to pay.
3. Negotiated and reduced payments with creditors.
4. Communicated with your creditors your inability to pay.
5. Stopped the harassing phone calls.
6. Placed yourself and your family on a budget.
7. If possible, obtained a part-time job or started a business.
8. Identified areas where you can reduce expenses.
9. Started building your emergency fund.

You will stay on this path until your residual income increases and allows you to start paying the creditors' on your "Pay-U-Latter List". This course you are on can last a year - stay the course. When you are ready to address your "pay you latter list", you will need two things. A copy of your credit report to know who to is reporting what, and who to contact. You will also need to know how to negotiate settlements on these accounts. Once your accounts go into a collection status you are no longer able to negotiate with the original creditor. The original creditor has turned your account over to a collection agency. If you have not received correspondence from the collection agency/company on any particular account, you can call the original creditor and they will direct you to who you need to work with. The negotiating knowledge is important because you no longer have to pay the entire original debt. If your money does not allow you to remedy the original debt, agencies will accept a settlement. It is better for your credit to pay the original debt, however, something is better than nothing, settle if you must.

Please note, if there is a "charge-off" on your credit report leave it alone. The debt has been written off and the creditor is no longer collecting. Don't dispute, don't inquire, don't pay, leave it alone.

Negotiating Settlements with Your Creditors/Debt Collectors

When you begin to pay off your debt, start with the most recent collection that has been reported on your credit report. By addressing the most recent negative reporting or your report, you are resolving those accounts that are effecting your credit score the most. Your credit report will tell you when each debt was last reported. The newer the collection the more damage it is doing to your credit score. If you are married and your resources only allow you to work on one person's debts at a time, let it be the one who generates the most income. As I said, you will need a copy of your credit report. You can request your free annual report online, by phone, or by mail.

On Line: AnnualCreditReport.com

By Phone: 1-877-322-8228

By Mail: Annual Credit Report
              Request Service
              P.O. Box 105281
              Atlanta, GA 30348-5281

When you request your free credit report you have the option of requesting reports from all three reporting agencies, equifax, experian, transunion, or order one report at a time. I strongly suggest that you request all three. You need to know what bureau is reporting what debts. Not all creditors report to all three bureaus, therefore you need all three**. (The free credit report does not come with a score. Your scored credit report is obtained only at a cost).** If you get a site that charges you a fee to obtain your free report, you are at the wrong site. Free means free! You are entitled to one free report every 12 months from each Bureau.

Once you have your credit reports, organize the collection companies by "date last reported", with the most recent reporting's first. Identify any agency that is collecting for more than one creditor. For example, you may see that ABC Company is showing three collections for three different creditors. When you contact ABC Company they will pull up all the accounts that they are collecting for, that is attached to your social security number. *(If any collection is seven years old, based on date of last activity, you need to note it as, uncollectable <u>and you will not pay or deal with that account now.</u> Later you will address these. Do not add these accounts to your organized list. The seven years is dated from the date you last made a payment to that creditor.)*

Once you have the collection agencies organized, add up the amount that each company is looking to collect. Make certain you don't have any duplicate collections. Sometimes ABC will be collecting for Credit Card Comp A but EFG collection agency originally had your account and sold it to ABC, but EFG is still showing on your credit report as a collection. Organizing your report will allow you to know how much money you will need before calling that particular agency.

Most collection agencies will settle for 50% of the original debt. Don't call until you have at least 50% of the debt. Work on resolving one creditor at a time. Be flexible, if you owe $2,000 and they offer to settle for $1,100, it's a good deal take the offer. If the balance is under $100.00 usually there is no negotiation.

Don't let collection agencies lure you into conversations regarding your income, what happened to cause you not to pay the debt etc. Keep them on the subject. You called to negotiate a settlement, not to discuss what caused you to get into your situation. If they want over 60% of the debt, say thank you and hang up. They now have your number, **they will call you back. DON'T PAY BEFORE YOU KNOW HOW YOU WILL RECEIVE PROOF OF SETTLEMENT.** You will need proof of payment for future reference, and a verbal agreement is not acceptable. I cannot stress this enough. It is not unheard of to hear a individual state that the ABC Company agreed to settle for X dollars however, when the client reviewed their credit report the debt was still showing as an active collection. When the Collection agency was contacted, of course, they had no record of the agreement, and the person you spoke to either did not exist or was no longer employed. Get it in writing! One alternative to settling without correspondence from the creditor is paying by mail. When you send the payment make sure your note on the subject line "PAID IN FULL FOR BLUE CREDIT CARD #1234544"

Do's And Don'ts When Negotiating A Settlement

1. Do not enter into negotiations until you have the funds to pay the debt.
2. Don't give your checking, debt, or savings account number for monthly drafts.
3. Pay by mail with notation of Paid In Full.
4. Make the agreed upon payment with a verifiable instrument such as a personal check, Western Union, Money Gram, Postal money order or Certified check.
5. If using money orders, only use Postal money Orders, they are easier to trace if lost.
6. Do what you agree to do.
7. Keep a folder with all the correspondence and proof of payment from all the Agencies you worked with. You will need this info to complete your debt crisis process.

You will stay on this course until you have resolved all your accounts you have chosen to pay. Your consumer credit history goes back many years. Any negative collection that is on your report that is seven years old must be removed by law, whether you paid it or not. The only exceptions to this are judgments and tax liens, that can stay on your report for ten years or more.

Each creditor that you pay off is **suppose** to report the resolution to the credit bureaus. You cannot trust what they are supposed to do.

You must make certain that your report has been updated. Once you have resolved **_all_** the accounts on your credit report, it is time to revisit your credit report. This time when you get your credit report, you want to also get the **scores** from all three bureaus. A credit report with scores can be obtained for free from some sites offering "free credit reports". However, when you are requesting TransUnion, Experion, or Equifax to update an error on your credit report they will want you to reference the report you purchased from them. So, go straight to the three credit bureaus and get your actual report. Each bureau will inform you of their cost. Review your report for errors. These errors can include:

1. Accounts that you have paid or settled, but still show as a collection.
2. Duplicate collections for the same account.
3. Collections that are over seven years old.
4. Account you never opened.
5. Erroneous late payments.

Now, the folder with all your correspondence and proof of settlement is very important. Identify all your errors and communicate to the appropriate bureau, requesting your information be corrected. When writing the letter you must reference the credit report you recently purchased. Each bureau should receive the letter detailing only the debts they are reporting. See sample letter.

> *Mr. Debt Freeman*
> *1111 One Road*
> *New Life, Debt USA*
> *SSN: 111 11 1111*
> *DOB: 01/01/47 Contact Number: 125-121-1212*
> *Reference: Equifax credit report # xxxxxx*
>
> *I have reviewed my most recent credit report and there are several errors. I have attached a copy of the report and detailed below the discrepancies. I have also attached proof of payment for these accounts.*

Creditor	Account#	Discrepancy
ABC Company	111111	paid 01/01
XZ Company	12121212	10yrs old
EFG Company	010101	paid 2/02

The BUGU Company is collecting for a debt that was originally with the MUGU Company. I settled this debt in June of 2009

HIRATE Company is collecting for a debt that was with the STRESSUOUT Company. I paid this account in July of 2009

I have enclosed a copy of my most recent light bill and my driver's license as proof of my residence and identity .

(One of the credit bureaus request proof of residence. Send it to each bureau you contact.)

Please update my credit report and send me an updated copy.

Thank You,

Since the last checkup you should have:

1. Obtained a copy of your free Credit Report and organized your debts and negotiated settlements with the creditors you placed on your "Pay-U-Latter List".
2. You have paid for an updated copy of your credit report with the scores from each bureau, identified errors, and communicated these errors to the credit bureaus and requested that they correct your report and send you an updated copy.
3. You have received your updated copy of your credit report from the three bureaus and rechecked for errors.

Once you receive your updated credit report you are now ready to begin the last phase, repairing your credit scores.

CHAPTER 2

YOUR CREDIT CRISIS

REPAIRING/RAISING YOUR CREDIT SCORES

IMPORTANT NOTE! IF YOUR ONLY CONCERN IS RAISING YOUR CREDIT SCORE, YOU SHOULD IMPLEMENT THIS CHAPTER AFTER YOU HAVE ESTABLISHED YOUR BUDGET AND BEFORE YOU START ANY DEBT NEGOTIATIONS/SETTLEMENTS. THE REASON FOR THIS IS THAT NEW CREDIT IS CRITICAL TO INCREASING ONES CREDIT SCORE. AND YOU WANT TO GET TO A TWO YEAR HISTORY ON EACH NEW LINE ON CREDIT AS SOON AS POSSIBLE.

Your credit did not become poor credit overnight, and it will not become good credit overnight. There is no quick resolution. Only time, new credit, and paying your new creditors on time, and resolving old debts, will give you a truly revitalized credit score. I cannot encourage you enough to not pay any credit repair company that claims to wipe out all your derogatory credit from your credit report by disputing everything on your credit report. The only way to restore your credit is to address each creditor/collection agency on your report and establishing new credit. A credit report is a factual account of your use of credit over the years. Anyone who offers to skew the facts of your history is offering to lie for you.

When an individual disputes items on their credit report the credit bureau sends this dispute to the creditor. The creditor that is reporting the debt has 30 days to respond to the credit bureau as to whether this is a valid debt. If the creditor does not respond within the time frame, the credit bureau removes that item from your credit report. If you have paid someone to dispute everything on your report, for that month, your scores may go up. But the following month or the month after, when the creditor re-reports that <u>accurate</u> information, your scores are back in the toilet, and the money you paid the credit repair company went in the same direction. Furthermore, when you do get your credit back on track, and say you are looking at purchasing a home. When mortgage lenders see that you disputed everything on your credit report, will need to prove them erroneous through the credit bureau doing an update, or pay them prior to you purchasing a home!

A creditable credit repair company/person will review your credit report with you, counsel you, and be your negotiator if you choose. They will tell you how to negotiate on your own, and how to establish new credit.

Credit Repair Companies should:

1. Present you with a contract outlining their fees and services.
2. Collect money only after a service has been rendered.
3. Instruct you on what must be done to get your credit back on track.
4. Inform you that you can perform all task on your own.

If you perceive that you have no use for a "good credit score" in the future, you can skip this step. However, if you are looking at educational loans for yourself or your children, real-estate loans, auto loans, government licensing, employment or business loans in the future, you will need a good credit score.

You want to get your credit scores as high as possible, 850 is the highest score. In this financial climate two bureaus reporting scores of 680 is considered good, but you can maneuver in the credit world with scores of 640. In order to raise your credit score you need a credit history that shows existing credit that has been paid as agreed for two years, and collections showing satisfied or settled. If you have no active accounts on your credit report you must establish new accounts. Its simple, active credit equals a credit score. No credit no score.

New accounts will start to affect your score approximately after six months of reporting. Lenders typically want to see four active lines of credit that have been active for 12-24 months. When establishing new accounts, establish these accounts as joint if you are married. Joint accounts will build each other's credit score. There are a few ways to establish new credit when your current credit will not allow you to obtain credit. The two options I will discuss are Secured Credit Cards and Secured loans.

Secured Credit Cards

Some local banks offer this type of card. If you can't find a local bank that offers Secured Credit Cards you will find many offers online. The secured credit card gives you a credit limit based on how much you deposit in an account. What you deposit is your credit limit. Understand, you are not going to like most of the offers online, but it is a means to an end. When looking online read, read, read. Know and understand all the fees associated with setting up the card. Select the card with the lowest fees. The interest rate is not a huge factor because you are not going to be carrying a balance. Paying the bill in its entirety, and on time, eliminates any interest charge, therefore interest rate is a mute point.

Once you have this card set up, don't lose sight of the fact that this is to build your credit score, not for you to have an extension of available credit and go into debt. Use the card infrequently and pay it off when the bill comes. Instead of paying cash for your gas put one fill up on your credit card and file it away until the bill is paid. You can set up more than one secured credit card and alternate usage. If you can't pay it off when the bill comes don't charge it.

Your scores can be effected in the negative if you charge over 50% of your credit limit. If you have a $500.00 limit and charge $351.00, your scores can go down. The credit scoring entities are not people but computers. These computers use various types of data, supplied by your creditors, to come up with your credit score. When the computer sees you have charged over 50% of your credit card limit it says; "She/he is overspending, they are getting ready to get out of control! Put up some safe guards, inhibit their ability to borrow, lower their score". It doesn't really say it like that, but you get the point! Stay below 50% of your limit on all your credit cards. Remember, if you are married, your accounts should be joint. Make one person the primary on account A, and make the other person primary on account B. This will allow for two new lines of credit on each of your credit reports.

Secured Bank Loans

Secured bank loans work a little different than secured credit cards. Most banks have a minimum loan amount of $1,000.00. Identify which banks offer secured loans. You go to bank #1 and ask for a secured loan. They take your $1,000 and put it in an account that cannot be accessed by you until the loan is paid off.

At the end of the loan process. Bank #1 will give you a check for $1,000, your loan. You can now take that same money to bank #2 and #3. At the end of the day you will still have $1,000.00, and you just added three new lines of credit to your credit report.

Each month that you pay the note, a portion of money is freed. You can allow this money to accumulate, and within three months, start using that money to make the payments. By doing this you will not have to worry about making another payment on the loan. It is like "set it and forget it".

Do not pay these accounts off early. You want the longest payment schedule possible because good reporting equals good credit source.

Revisit Your Credit Report

After twelve months from the time you made your first payment on your secured loan and credit card, check and see what your credit score is. When you receive your credit report, again look for errors. For each error, go through the process as outlined previously. You can test to see if you are now credit worthy without getting your credit report by applying for a regular credit card. If you are approved, you know that your scores have risen to an acceptable level of creditworthiness. Once you are able to get credit through regular channels you no longer need the secured credit card. However, if you obtain a regular credit card *do not cancel the secured cards until you have had the new credit card for twelve months. Also, don't pay-off the secured loans early. Let them run their course. Renewing the secured loans will continue to help your score.*

Credit Bureau Contact Information

Equifax
P.O. Box 740241
Atlanta, GA 30374-0541
800-685-1111

Experian
P.O. Box 2002
Allen, TX 75013
888-397-3742

TransUnion
P.O. Box 1000
Chester,PA 19022
800 888 4213

Federal Trade Commission
Consumer Response Center FCRA,
Federal Trade Commission
Washington, DC 20580
877-382-4357

What is a FICO score?

FICO - Fair Issac Corp., was founded in 1956 by Bill Fair, an engineer, and Earl Issac, a mathematician, who developed the FICO scores. The FICO scores tells a creditor your degree of credit risk. The scores are generated by utilizing various information that has been generated by creditors you have interacted with. Below you will see what information makes up your score.

What is used when Generating your score	Percent of the effect on your credit score
Payment history	35%
Amount owed on debts	30%
How long have you had account	15%
New Accounts	10%
Types of credit	10%

What can negatively impact your score:

1. Maxing out a credit card.
2. Owing more than 50% on the total of your allowable credit cards.
3. Paying 30 days late on any debt.

4. Settling a debt for less than the original amount. (I know I encouraged you to settle your debts, it is a necessary means to an end. Paying something is better than paying nothing.)
5. Foreclosure.
6. Bankruptcy.
7. Allowing negative inform to stay on your report that is older than 7 years.
8. Excessive inquiries.
9. No credit or limited credit history.

Having a 30 day late reported to the bureaus' can lower your score up to 100 points. Creditors do not report 28 days late or 29 days late, they report when your are 30 day late. So don't go over 30 days late on any debt.

CHAPTER 3

DEBT ESCALATION

Getting out of debt is probably everyone's goal. Imagine, its payday and all you have to do is pay for your mortgage/rent, utilities and put food in the home and your various insurances. It is possible! Below I have extracted some of the debts from the debt worksheet in Chapter one. The following scenario is based on all debt originating January 2010.

Debt/Expenses Total($) Paid	Owe($)	Min. Pymt$	Yrs to Pay-off	Interest Paid($)
Mortgage 352,690.37	155,000	979.71	30	197,690.37
2nd Mtg. 54,007.84	25,000	300.04	15	29,007.84
Car 21,092.81	18,000	439.43	4	3,092.81
Gas Card 2,124.64	1,000	27.50	9.9	1,124.64
Card 3,173.25	1,500	37.50	12.75	1,673.25
Totals($) 433,088.91	200,500	1,784.18	30	232,588.91

As you can see by paying only the minimum payment on your debt after 30 years you would have paid back $433,088.91 for a starting debt of $200,500.

Look at the Gas Card debt of $1,000, see why it is going to take 9.9 years to pay it off? As you make your payment of $27.50, only $10.00 goes towards the principal. And because you only make a minimum payment, your minimum requirement for the next month goes down along with the amount that is going towards your remaining balance. I have displayed only the first 24 months.

Month	Minimum Payment	Interest Paid	Principal Paid	Remaining Balance
1	$27.50	$17.50	$10.00	$990.00
2	$27.22	$17.33	$9.90	$980.11
3	$26.95	$17.15	$9.80	$970.31
4	$26.68	$16.98	$9.70	$960.61
5	$26.42	$16.81	$9.61	$951.00
6	$26.15	$16.64	$9.51	$941.49
7	$25.89	$16.48	$9.41	$932.08
8	$25.63	$16.31	$9.32	$922.76
9	$25.38	$16.15	$9.23	$913.53
10	$25.13	$15.99	$9.14	$904.39
11	$24.87	$15.83	$9.04	$895.35
12	$24.62	$15.67	$8.95	$886.40
13	$24.37	$15.51	$8.86	$877.54
14	$24.14	$15.36	$8.78	$868.76
15	$23.89	$15.20	$8.69	$860.07
16	$23.65	$15.05	$8.60	$851.47
17	$23.41	$14.90	$8.51	$842.96
18	$23.18	$14.75	$8.43	$834.53
19	$22.95	$14.60	$8.35	$826.18
20	$22.72	$14.46	$8.26	$817.92
21	$22.49	$14.31	$8.18	$809.74
22	$22.27	$14.17	$8.10	$801.64
23	$22.05	$14.03	$8.02	$793.62
24	$21.83	$13.89	$7.94	$785.68

Escalating debt takes time, and patience. I have reorganized the debts above from the smallest bill to the largest. As you go through the process you must commit to spending the same amount of money, or more, on your bills each month until the last debt is paid. In the example below, the individual will be debt free in 16 years including the mortgage, by adding $50.00 to his current debt. When the first debt is paid off that payment will be added to the next debt. This process will continue until all debts are paid.

Debt	Balance($)	Min.($) Pymt.	Scheduled Pay-off	Increased Payment($)	Total Pymt. ($)	New pay off
1.	Gas Card					
	1,000	27.50	9/2019	50.00	77.50	4/2011

Paid off in 1.3 yrs. By adding $50.00 to your minimum payment.

2.	Gas Card					
	1,200	33.00	5/2021	77.50	110.5	3/2012

After 1.3 yrs. you will still owe $1,032.08.

By adding $77.50 to your minimum payment of $33.00 you will pay this off in 2.3 years.

3.	Store Card					
	1,500	37.50	8/2022	110.50	148.00	12/2012

After 2.3 years you still owe $1,155.08.

By adding $110.50 to your minimum payment of $37.50 You will pay this off in 2.11 yrs.

4.	Car					
	18,000	439.43	1/2014	148.00	587.43	8/2013

After 2.11 yrs. you still owe $5,855.09.

By adding $148.00 to your minimum payment of $439.43 you will pay this off in 3.8 yrs.

5.	2nd Mortgage					
	25,000	300.04	1/2025	587.43	887.47	1/2016

After 3.8 yrs. you still owe $22,327.87.

By adding $587.43 to your minimum payment of $300.04 or, or by making One annual payment of $7,049.16 ($300.04x12), you will pay off your 2nd mortgage in 6 yrs.

6.	1st Mortgage					
	155,000	979.71	1/2040	887.47	1867.18	11/2024

After 6 years you still owe $142,701.

By adding $887.47 to your payment of $979.71 or, by making one annual payment of $10,649.64 ($979.71x12), you will pay off this mortgage in 14.11 yrs.

CHAPTER 4

YOUR MORTGAGE CRISIS

Contrary to some beliefs, mortgage companies do not want your home, regardless of how much equity you have in it. When you are in trouble with your mortgage, your mortgage company is your best friend. Your best friend has a few options they can offer you to help you out of your crisis that fall under "Loan Modification".

1. They can place you in the Making Home Affordable Program. This is a Federal Government sponsored program. The program takes your current mortgage, lowers the interest rate and lowers your payment. There are some qualifiers most lenders require you to meet to be considered for this program:
    a. There has to have been a financial hardship. Examples: Has there been a change in income in the household due to job loss, death, divorce etc.
    b. You are paying greater than 31% of your gross income toward your mortgage. The 31% includes your principal payment, taxes, and home owner's insurance and Homeowner Association dues. It does not include your Mortgage Insurance Payments on an existing loan.(MI or Mortgage Insurance is a fee on FHA loans.)
    c. The loan must be on your primary residence
    d. You must owe less than $729,750.00

e. Your original loan must have been generated before January 2009.

2. They can put you on a Payment Plan. Under the payment plan the mortgage company will take the payments you are behind, and spread this amount out over a period of time. That amount will be added to your current mortgage until you have paid all the arrears. In essence, you will have a higher mortgage payment until the arrears are paid.

3. They can modify your loan. In this scenario they refinance your loan with a new 30 year fixed loan.

Call your mortgage company and ask to be connected the Making Homes Affordable department. Take notes, know who you speak to, when, and what they said. You will be required to gather and send a number of documents. Don't delay, and stay in contact with your mortgage company once you have sent the documents.

During this process, which can take several months to complete, make certain that your homeowners insurance and taxes are paid if not included in your mortgage. If your taxes and insurance payments are not included in your mortgage make sure your mortgage company has evidence that you have paid these two expenses. If you have not paid taxes and insurance, usually, your Lender will pay your taxes and "Force Place" insurance on your property, this insurance only cover the structure not the contents. In the event of a loss, the Lender gets paid, not you. While going through the Modification process save your mortgage payments money if your mortgage company will not accept your payments at this time. In either the Making Home Affordable Program or a Modification that spreads out your arrears over time, you may be required to submit a lump sum that goes towards the arrears.

Regardless of how far behind you are on your mortgage, even if you have received a "Notice of intent to foreclose, you still have the opportunity to get a loan modification from your mortgage company. ***Don't pay any company to do a modification for you unless the fee is paid when the modification is complete!*** When you are in a crisis with your mortgage, talk to your mortgage company. You and your mortgage company can achieve your desired goals without the interaction of a third party and most importantly, without any upfront fees. Most Loan Modification Companies charge a fee to do what you can do for free.

Most recently States have been given bail-out money for homeowners. Contact your state government for their program guidelines. This program charges no fees and will work with you to get you current or restructure your loan.

Your Foreclosure Crisis

Foreclosure proceedings typically do not start until you are three months behind on your mortgage, I said typically! When you get three months behind on your mortgage payment, your mortgage company generally will only accept the full amount of the arrears. (At this point, if you see that you will continue to have this hardship, apply for a modification.)

If modification has failed and your mortgage company attorney has sent you foreclosure papers you will be informed of a hearing. Go to the hearing! At the hearing you will have an opportunity to present your situation. The worst case scenario is that you will be informed of a sale date. At this point the only way to stop the sale of your home is to pay the arrears or file a Chapter 13 bankruptcy. If you file a Chapter 13, remember **the entire mortgage** may **not** go in the Chapter 13, just what is past due, the arrears.

A Chapter 13 is going to add additional debt. First you have to pay an attorney to file the Chapter 13. Once it is filed, you will now have a mortgage payment and a Chapter 13 payment.

If filing is your only option and you have a great deal of long term consumer debt, include all your debt in the filing. Including all your debt may reduce your total monthly payments. This can occur because all debt payments are negotiated for lower payments by your plan administrator for your Chapter 13. This next statement is Very, Very important to remember. **Missing either your regular mortgage payment or your chapter 13 payment, will allow the mortgage company to petition the court to be removed from the Chapter 13, and the foreclosure will start again from where it left off at, the sale.** If your property goes to sale you have up until the morning of the sale to pay the arrears to the attorney that is representing the mortgage company. During the foreclosure process, you can still be speaking with your mortgage company and asking for a modification. I encourage you to stay in contact with the mortgage company and more importantly, the attorney that is handling the foreclosure. Once an agreement has been reached regarding the mortgage company, the attorney is the responsible party that must stop the sale. Make sure he/she has been contacted by your mortgage company and that they are going to take the appropriate action and when.

CHAPTER 5

BACK ON TRACK

Once you get on track stay on track. Use credit wisely. Once you get your credit on track and you don't want to use credit cards you can continue with the secured bank loans to build your credit score, but having at least one credit card really helps your score.

1. Live on a budget.
2. Don't live above your means.
3. Create an emergency fund - save 6-12 months' worth of bills/ cost of living in a do not touch account.
4. Begin a routine savings.
5. If you are married, have three checking accounts, and four savings accounts.
    a. Checking account #1 - only the bills are paid out of this account
    b. Checking account #2&3 - Each of you should have your own Checking account to spend as you please - NO QUESTIONS ASKED.
    c. Savings #1 - account for your emergency fund.
    d. Savings #2 - One joint long term savings account.
    e. Savings #3&4 each of you have one personal savings accounts NO QUESTIONS ASKED ACCOUNT - YOUR MONEY.
6. Don't have a debit card attached to your savings accounts.
7. Max out your investments in your retirement plans.

8. Start investing to obtain larger returns on your long term savings.

These steps will keep you out of chaos when a financial crisis arises. Also, if you are married and follow all the steps in number five above, money will never be an issue in your home.

Building Your Children's Credit

This is really, really simple. Once your child becomes legal, you want to help them establish credit. If you are buying them a car THAT YOU ARE PAYING FOR, add them to the loan. Add them as authorized users on your credit cards. Get them credit cards in their name only, but you keep the card in your possession. Allow the card out of your sight for designated purchases, and when the bill comes pay it. Educate them about the consequences of not paying their bills on time, amassing debt and not having an emergency fund. Encourage them to save for future purchases and be patient when it comes to their desires. Caution them on the negative impact of the "buy now pay latter syndrome". Once they are gainfully employed, paying their bills, pass on their credit cards to them. By you establishing their credit as teenagers, they will enter the world as a young adult with great credit scores. And most importantly, when they are preparing to move out on their own make sure you give them a copy of this book.

CHAPTER 6

A SPIRITUAL PERSPECTIVE REGARDING YOUR DEBT CRISIS

For those of us who are Christians, we are called to a higher standard when it comes to managing God's money that He has entrusted to us. When we are in a Debt Crisis we can look back and see that we have partly arrived in the situation due to our disobedience to one or more of God's principals, as it relates to money. Below I have listed a few reminders to help keep you on course, once you get back on track. We are stewards, caretakers of the things that God gives us. We all have veered off the course of the street called "God's way". Isn't it so good to know that He allows u-turns!

1. Are you giving at least 10% of your income for the work of God, which is the tithe? If you are not tithing, you are robbing God and you are not in order with His financial principal nor are we demonstrating our faith and trust in his Word, and thereby not positioning ourselves to receive His promises.

Malachi 3:10: "Bring ye all the tithes into the storehouse, that there may be meat in mine house, and prove me now herewith, saith the Lord of hosts, if I will not open you the windows of heaven, and pour you out a blessing, that there shall not be room enough to receive it."

2. Are you giving with joy or regret?

2 Corinthians 9:6-8: "But this I say, He which soweth sparingly shall reap also sparingly; and he which soweth bountifully shall reap also bountifully. Every man according as he purposeth in his heart, so let him give; not grudgingly, or of necessity: for God loveth a cheerful giver. And God is able to make all grace abound toward you; that ye, always having all sufficiency in all things, may abound to every good work."

3. When you make your budget or pay your bills, what is the first item? Is it your tithe?

Proverbs 3:9-10: "Honour the Lord with thy substance, and with the firstfruits of all thine increase: So shall thy barns be filled with plenty, and thy presses shall burst out with new wine."

4. Are you planning for future expenditures wisely to avoid going into debt?

Luke 14:28-30: "For which of you, intending to build a tower, sitteth not down first, and counteth the cost, whether he have sufficient to finish it? Lest haply, after he hath laid the foundation, and is not able to finish it, all that behold it begin to mock him, Saying, This man began to build, and was not able to finish."

5. Are you lazy? Lazy individuals will not prosper. Whether it is in the maintenance of your home or on your prospective jobs, laziness is an ill that will permeate every aspect of your life, and cause no good thing to be sustained in your life.

Proverbs 21:25 "The desire of the slothful killeth him; for his hands refuse to labour."

6. God does not want you in debt.

Romans 13:8: "Owe no man anything, but to love one another: for he that loveth another hath fulfilled the law."

7. Do you fast and pray regarding your finances?

Isaiah 58:6 & 9: "Is not this the fast that I have chosen? to loose the bands of wickedness, to undo the heavy burdens, and to let the oppressed go free, and that ye break every yoke? Then shalt thou call, and the Lord shall answer; thou shalt cry, and he shall say, Here I am. If thou take away from the midst of thee the yoke, the putting forth of the finger, and speaking vanity"

8. Before making a financial decision do you seek Gods wisdom and understanding regarding the matter?

Proverbs 24:3-4: "Through wisdom is an house builded; and by understanding it is established: And by knowledge shall the chambers be filled with all precious and pleasant riches."

9. Storms and hard times will come. How we conduct ourselves in the mist of those storms and hard times, is our demonstration of our faith and trust in God displayed. It is hard, yes hard to be thankful in every season of your life. However, if we never lose sight of who is in control, our ability to be thankful while we are going through is enhanced. We should be totally committed and thankful to God, no matter what is happening, because we have the confidence that He will direct us through any and all situations.

Philippians 4:4-7: "Rejoice in the Lord always: and again I say, Rejoice. Let your moderation be known unto all men. The Lord is at hand. Be careful for nothing; but in everything by prayer and supplication with thanksgiving let your requests be made known unto God. And the peace of God, which passeth all understanding, shall keep your hearts and minds through Christ Jesus."

10. Are we seeking financial blessing instead of seeking God and His will? Are we wanting the benefits that God has for us but not wanting to conduct ourselves in a manner he has ordained?

Matthew 15:8: "This people draweth nigh unto me with their mouth, and honoureth me with their lips; but their heart is far from me."

11. To receive increase you must demonstrate you ability to manage your finances of today.

Matthew 25:21, "His lord said unto him, Well done, thou good and faithful servant: thou hast been faithful over a few things, I will make thee ruler over many things: enter thou into the joy of thy Lord.

CONCLUSION

MAY YOU NOT CHARGE AND PROSPER

WORKSHEETS

Debt/Expenses Work Sheet

Total Take Home Pay _____

Debt and Expenses

Debt/Expenses		Owe($)	Payment($)
1.	Tithe		_____
2.	Mortgage/Rent	_____	_____
3.	2nd Mortgage	_____	_____
4.	Loans Credit Cards		
	a. _____	_____	_____
	b. _____	_____	_____
	c. _____	_____	_____
	d. _____	_____	_____
	e. _____	_____	_____
	f. _____	_____	_____
	g. _____	_____	_____
	h. _____	_____	_____
5.	Car #1	_____	_____
6.	Car #2	_____	_____
7.	Car Insurance		_____
8.	Life Insurance		_____
9.	Food/home supplies		_____

10. Utilities   _____
11. Gas Cars   _____
12. Phones   _____
13. _____   _____
14. _____   _____
15. _____   _____
16. _____   _____
17. _____   _____
18. _____   _____

Debt and Expenses

Debt/Expenses	Owe($)	Payment($)

19. Residual Expenses
    a. Hair cuts   _____
    b. _____   _____
    c. _____   _____
    d. _____   _____
    e. _____   _____
    f. _____   _____
    g. _____   _____

Totals   _____

Shortfall or Residual Income

Income minus total expenses:_____

Pay-U-Later List/Reduced Payment Request

Creditor	Regular Payment	Negotiated Payment	Pay-U-Latter Letter Sent
_____	_____	_____	_____
_____	_____	_____	_____
_____	_____	_____	_____
_____	_____	_____	_____
_____	_____	_____	_____
_____	_____	_____	_____
_____	_____	_____	_____
_____	_____	_____	_____
_____	_____	_____	_____
_____	_____	_____	_____
_____	_____	_____	_____
_____	_____	_____	_____
_____	_____	_____	_____
_____	_____	_____	_____
_____	_____	_____	_____

Budget Work Sheet

To be completed after you complete your Pay-u-Latter List

Available Funds   _____

Debt/Expenses	Owe($)	Payment($)
1. Tithe		_____
2. Emergency Fund		_____
3. Long term Savings		_____
4. Mortgage/Rent	_____	_____
5. 2nd Mortgage	_____	_____
6. Loans Credit Cards		
a. _____	_____	_____
b. _____	_____	_____
c. _____	_____	_____
d. _____	_____	_____
e. _____	_____	_____
f. _____	_____	_____
g. _____	_____	_____
h. _____	_____	_____
7. Car #1	_____	_____
8. Car #2	_____	_____
9. Car Insurance		_____
10. Life Insurance		_____
11. Food/home supplies		_____
12. Utilities		_____
13. Gas Cars		_____
14. Phones		_____

15. _____ _____

16. _____ _____

17. _____ _____

18. Residual Expenses

    a. Hair cuts _____

    b. _____ _____

    c. _____ _____

    d. _____ _____

    e. _____ _____

    f. _____ _____

Totals _____

Residual or Shortfall - Funds minus payments _____

Debt Organizational/Negotiation
Worksheet from Credit Report

Creditor	Collection Company	Amount Owed	Negotiated Amount	Amount Saved	Date
_____	_____	____	____	____	__
_____	_____	____	____	____	__
_____	_____	____	____	____	__
_____	_____	____	____	____	__
_____	_____	____	____	____	__
_____	_____	____	____	____	__
_____	_____	____	____	____	__
_____	_____	____	____	____	__
_____	_____	____	____	____	__
_____	_____	____	____	____	__
_____	_____	____	____	____	__
_____	_____	____	____	____	__
_____	_____	____	____	____	__
_____	_____	____	____	____	__
_____	_____	____	____	____	__

Debt Escalation Worksheet

Creditor	Amount Owed	Payment	Expected Payoff Date	Escalated Amount	Start New Date	Payoff Date

Author Contact for speaking engagement/assistance:

A. Nellie Bloedoorn
ASFS1952@aol.com